Zoom in on
MAKING DECISIONS
AS A GROUP

Rita Santos

E **Enslow Publishing**
101 W. 23rd Street
Suite 240
New York, NY 10011
USA

enslow.com

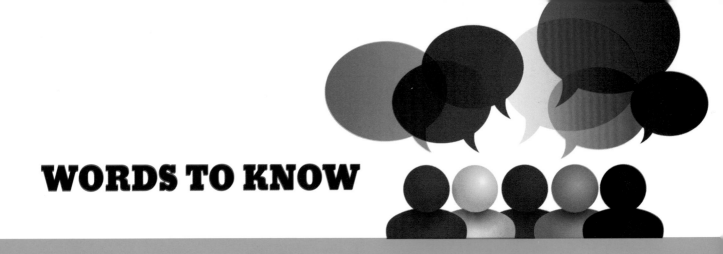

WORDS TO KNOW

bipartisan Involving the agreement and cooperation of two or more political parties.

citizen A member of a community or nation.

compromise To settle an argument by each side giving up something.

consensus An agreement.

democracy A form of government in which all citizens have a voice.

empathy The ability to understand the feelings of others.

majority More than half of a group.

petition A document that people sign when they want someone to change something.

quorum The minimum number of members of a group needed to make a decision.

senator A person who represents his or her state or district in government.

veto To reject a decision.

CONTENTS

Making Decisions as a Group

Life is made of choices. Every day we decide lots of different things, like what to have for breakfast or where to sit on the bus. These kinds of decisions can be easy because they only affect you. Decisions that affect multiple people are usually made in groups. Some groups are made of only a few people and some are very large. The ability for citizens to make decisions about their government is part of what makes America a democracy. Being able to make decisions as a group is a civic virtue.

Our Roles as Citizens

As citizens, we have a responsibility to act in a way that makes our communities nice and safe for everyone. Civic virtues are ideas or ways of behaving that are good for the whole community. Fair decision-making is a civic virtue. Decisions about how our communities should run are made in groups because they affect everyone.

Can We Agree?

A majority decision means more than 50 percent of people agree.

Good for Everyone

Making decisions can be hard because what's good for one person isn't always good for everyone. You may love peanut butter, but it's a dangerous food for someone who is allergic to peanuts. When we make decisions that affect a lot of people, we should make sure our choices won't harm anyone. Getting everyone to agree isn't easy, but learning how to work together is an important part of living in a democracy.

In town hall meetings like this one, citizens have a chance to give their opinions before decisions are made.

How to Make Decisions as a Group

When we make decisions as a group we must first discuss what the issue or problem is. Then we can figure out what's causing it and how we should fix it. Agreeing that something is a problem is usually much easier than agreeing on how to fix it. Most problems can be solved in a number of different ways. When people of different backgrounds work together on a problem they can usually come up with creative solutions.

Listening to each other is a key part of group decision making.

Learning to Listen

People make choices based on what they know about a problem and how it affects them. Part of making decisions as a group is learning to put ourselves in other people's shoes. Empathy is our ability to understand how and why

other people feel the way they do. Trying to understand others can help us figure out what's best for everyone.

The easiest way to understand people is to listen to what they have to say with an open mind. When you find yourself disagreeing with someone, try to imagine things from their point of view. It just might change how you view the issue.

Learning to Compromise

Complicated problems usually have complicated solutions. When people can agree on some parts of a solution but not

Roll Call

A quorum is the minimum number of members of an organization that must be present for a decision to be made.

others, it might be time for a compromise. Compromising is an important part of decision making. It means that each side keeps something they want and gives up something they want in order to reach an agreement. Some things, like the safety of people or the environment, should never be compromised.

Compromise is one of the best ways to reach decisions as a group.

Making Decisions at Home and School

We are all parts of lots of different groups. If you play sports, your team is a group. You and your friends from school make up another group. Even your family counts as a group! When you know a group of people well, it can be easier to work with them because you all understand each other. But even when you know people well, there can still be disagreements that you will need to work through.

Members of a team must work together to make the team as strong as possible.

Different Opinions Are Okay!

You and your friends probably like a lot of the same things, but even best friends disagree sometimes. You might love the same book but have different favorite characters. That's okay! Having a different opinion from someone else doesn't mean one person is right and the other is wrong. Talking to people with different opinions helps us see things from a different perspective—that's a great way to learn.

> ## No Way!
> **When Congress does not approve of a law they can veto it.**

For the Good of the Group

Sometimes making decisions as a group means putting aside your own feelings. Suppose your sports team is choosing a new team captain. One of the choices is your best friend. But is he really the best person for the job? Your teammates may have lots of different opinions. Take

People from different backgrounds can learn from each other by sharing their opinions.

the time to listen carefully to each opinion and decide who makes the strongest case. You want to choose the person who will do the best job for the team, even if it's not your best friend.

Making Decisions as Citizens

America is a representative democracy. That means we choose politicians to represent us. Politicians from every state work together to make decisions about what's best for the whole country. We vote for politicians when we agree with their ideas and values. It's important that we let our elected officials know what issues matter to us so that they can make decisions based on what the people in their community want. There are many ways we can do this. You can call, email, or write to your representative. It's their job to listen to you!

Members of the United States Congress are elected to represent all of the country's citizens.

Choosing Your Representative

Citizens choose politicians to make decisions about how the country should run. They do this by voting. Sometimes our representatives make small decisions, like what the state bird should be. Sometimes they make big decisions, like how to help families in need. No matter what kinds of decisions politicians make, they have to work to reach a consensus, even when they don't agree.

Across the Aisle

When members of more than one political party work together it is called a bipartisan effort.

Talking to Your Representative

A good politician can explain the decisions he makes. People feel better about decisions when they understand them. But sometimes people disagree with the choices their representatives make. When people feel like their representatives aren't listening, they may choose to start a petition or a protest.

America's founding fathers knew it was important for people to be able to

Voting is a great way to make your voice heard.

Citizens gather with their representative. They can help him make good decisions for their group.

gather in groups and discuss their issues. The First Amendment of the Constitution gives citizens the right to assemble and to ask their government to address issues. When people protest, it is a sign they feel unheard by their representatives and need to be listened to.

Making decisions in groups allows us to solve big problems. When people listen to each other they can come up with solutions that are good for everyone.

ACTIVITY: WRITE TO YOUR SENATOR

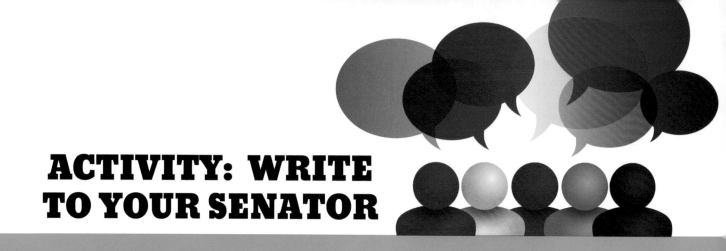

Choose one issue that is important to you. Research your issue online and at the library. Write a letter to your senator explaining what steps you think he or she should take on that issue and why it matters to you. Mail your letter!

Not sure where to send your letter? Go to www.USA.gov for a list of representatives for every state.

LEARN MORE

Books

Cavell-Clarke, Steffi. *Making Good Choices.* New York, NY: Crabtree Publishing Company, 2017.

Coan, Sharon. *Being a Good Citizen.* Huntington Beach, CA: Teacher Created Material, 2015.

Pegis, Jessica. *What Is Citizenship?* New York, NY: Crabtree Publishing Company, 2016.

Websites

The Constitution for Kids
Usconstitution.net/constkidsK
Learn the history of the United States Constitution and Bill of Rights.

What Is Democracy?
mocomi.com/what-is-democracy/
Find out more fun facts about what it means to live in a democracy.

INDEX

Published in 2019 by Enslow Publishing, LLC.
101 W. 23rd Street, Suite 240, New York, NY 10011

Copyright © 2019 by Enslow Publishing, LLC.
All rights reserved.

No part of this book may be reproduced by any means without the written permission of the publisher.

Library of Congress Cataloging-in-Publication Data

Names: Santos, Rita, author.
Title: Zoom in on making decisions as a group / Rita Santos.
Description: New York, NY : Enslow Publishing, [2019] | Series: Zoom in on civic virtues | Audience: Grades K-4. | Includes bibliographical references and index.
Identifiers: LCCN 2017047455| ISBN 9780766097759 (library bound) | ISBN 9780766097766 (pbk.) | ISBN 9780766097773 (6 pack)
Subjects: LCSH: Group decision making—Juvenile literature. | Civics—Juvenile literature.
Classification: LCC HM746 .S26 2018 | DDC 302.3—dc23
LC record available at https://lccn.loc.gov/2017047455

Printed in the United States of America

To Our Readers: We have done our best to make sure all website addresses in this book were active and appropriate when we went to press. However, the author and the publisher have no control over and assume no liability for the material available on those websites or on any websites they may link to. Any comments or suggestions can be sent by e-mail to customerservice@enslow.com.

Photo Credits: Cover, p. 1 wavebreakmedia/Shutterstock.com; p. 4 WAYHOME studio/Shutterstock.com; p. 7 Bill Pugliano/Getty Images; p. 9 ESB Professional/Shutterstock.com; p. 11 Monkey Business Images/Shutterstock.com; p. 12 pikselstock/Shutterstock.com; p. 14 SpeedKingz/Shutterstock.com; p. 16 Photographee.eu/Shutterstock.com; p. 18 Bill Clark/CQ-Roll Call Group/Getty Images; p. 20 Gino Santa Maria/Shutterstock.com; p. 21 Joseph Gruber/Shutterstock.com; p. 23 Sergey Maksienko/Shutterstock.com; illustrated people and talk balloons pp. 2, 3, 22, back cover KreativKolors/Shutterstock.com; illustrated children and puzzle pp. 5, 8, 13, 17 CuteCute/Shutterstock.com.